Published by Creative Education
P.O. Box 227, Mankato, Minnesota 56002
Creative Education is an imprint of
The Creative Company
www.thecreativecompany.us

Design and production by The Design Lab
Art direction by Rita Marshall
Printed in the United States of America

Photographs by Big Stock Photo (Mouskie),
Dreamstime (Ongchangwei), Getty Images (Gary
Bell, TORSTEN BLACKWOOD/AFP, Gerry Ellis, Tim
Graham, James Hager, ZZSD), iStockphoto (Jeremy
Edwards, Eric Isselee, Matthew Jones, Smiley Joanne,
Sawayasu Tsuji, Michael Willis)

Library of Congress Cataloging-in-Publication Data
Bodden, Valerie.
Koalas / by Valerie Bodden.
p. cm. — (Amazing animals)
Includes bibliographical references and index.
ISBN 978-1-58341-715-7
1. Koala—Juvenile literature. I. Title. II. Series.

QL737.M384B63 2009
599.2′5—dc22   2007051587

First Edition
9 8 7 6 5 4 3 2 1

AMAZING ANIMALS

KOALAS

BY VALERIE BODDEN

CREATIVE EDUCATION

Koalas are round, furry animals.
They are marsupials (*mar-SOO-pee-uhlz*).
That means that mother koalas have a
pouch on their belly to hold their babies.

*Koalas have big,
dark-colored noses*

Koalas have brown or gray fur. Their ears, arms, and chests are white. Koalas have big noses. They have strong feet and claws to help them climb.

Koalas have fuzzy-looking fur and hard claws

Some koalas are small. They weigh a little bit more than a newborn human baby. Other koalas are bigger. They can weigh up to 30 pounds (13.6 kg).

Koalas are small enough to easily climb trees

Australia has a lot of trees for koalas to live in

Koalas live on the continent of Australia. They live high in eucalyptus (*yoo-kuh-LIP-tus*) trees. Some of the trees are in the mountains. Others are on flat land.

continent one of Earth's seven big pieces of land

mountains very big hills made of rock

Koalas eat leaves, bark, and fruit from eucalyptus trees. They do not eat from any other kinds of trees. Koalas have a good sense of smell. It helps them find the best leaves to eat.

Many koalas eat three pounds (1.3 kg) of leaves a day

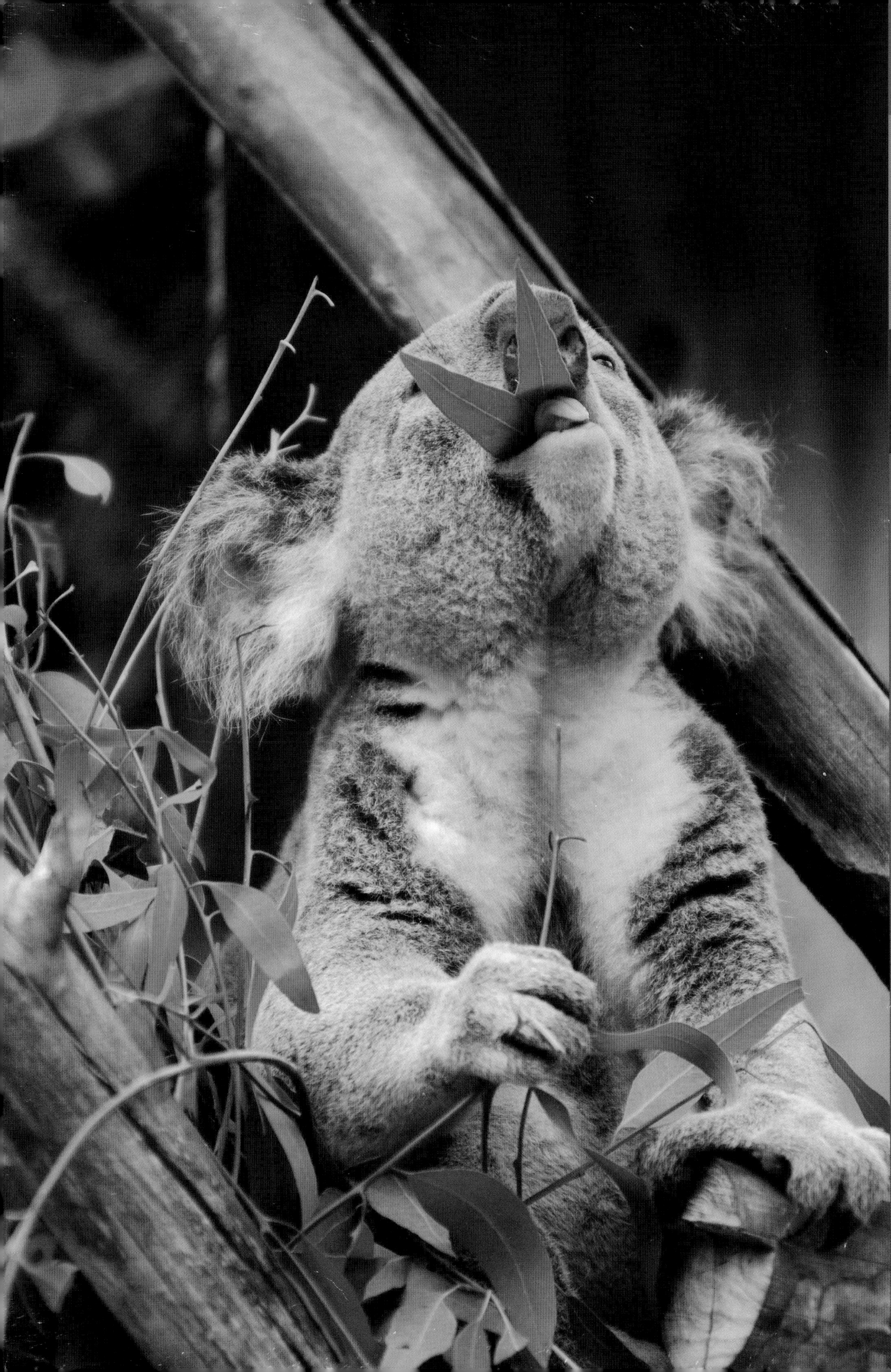

A joey lives in its mother's pouch for about six months

Most mother koalas have one **joey** at a time. The joey is the size of a jellybean when it is born! The joey crawls into its mother's pouch. When it gets bigger, it comes out. Koalas can live more than 10 years in the wild.

joey a baby koala

*Koala feet are better for
climbing than for walking*

Grown koalas live alone.

Each one has a **territory** of its own high
in the trees. Koalas stay in the trees most
of the time. But they come down once in
a while to move to a new tree.

territory an area that is the home of one animal

Koalas are most active at night. They move from branch to branch looking for leaves to eat. After they eat, koalas nap. They nap a lot! Koalas sleep 18 to 20 hours a day.

Koalas like to find branches where they can sleep

Many people around the world love koalas. Some people look for them when they visit Australia. Others go to see koalas in zoos. Even though they mostly just sleep and eat, these furry animals are fun to watch!

Koalas live in zoos in countries all over the world

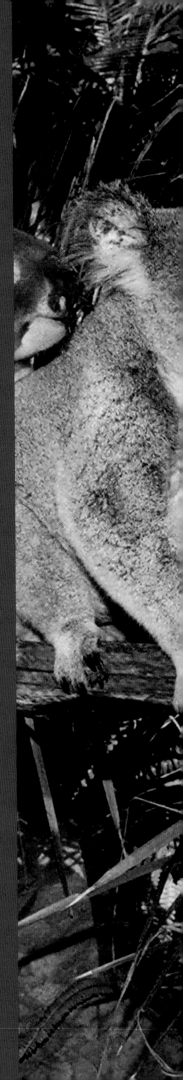

A Koala Story

Why don't koalas have tails? People in Australia used to tell a story about this. They said that once a koala and a kangaroo went to look for water. The kangaroo dug in the ground for water. The koala did not help. But when the kangaroo found water, the koala drank it. The kangaroo was so mad that he cut off the koala's tail. From then on, koalas did not have tails!

Read More

Pohl, Kathleen. *Koalas*. Milwaukee: Weekly Reader Early Learning Library, 2007.

Stone, Tanya Lee. *Koalas*. San Diego: Blackbirch, 2003.

Web Sites

Enchanted Learning: Koala
http://www.enchantedlearning.com/subjects/mammals/marsupial/Koalaprintout.shtml
This site has koala facts and a picture to color.

National Geographic Little Kids: Koala Family
http://littlekids.nationalgeographic.com/littlekids/animals/koala-family-1.html
This site tells about koala mothers and babies.

Index